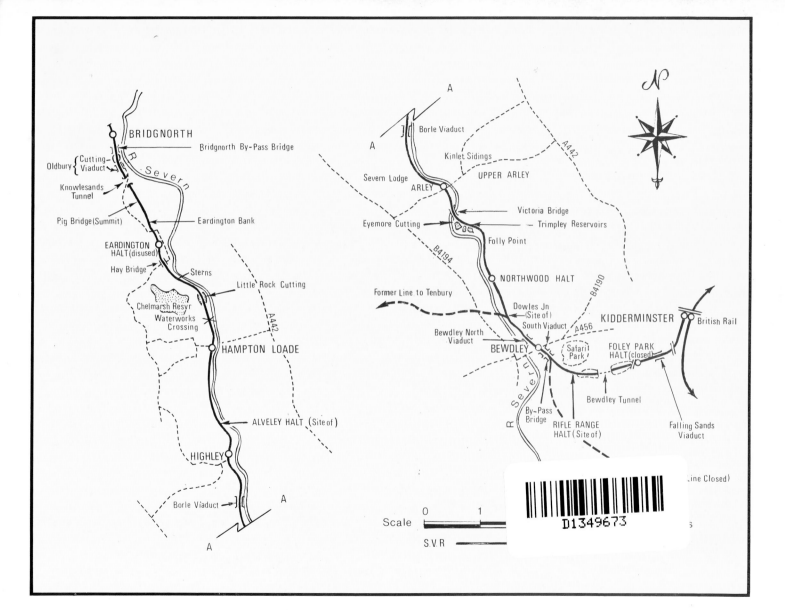

BRIDGNORTH

Bridgnorth By-Pass Bridge

Oldbury { Cutting
{ Viaduct

R. Severn

Knowlesands Tunnel

Pig Bridge (Summit)

Eardington Bank

EARDINGTON HALT (disused)

Hay Bridge

Sterns

Little Rock Cutting

Chelmarsh Resvr

Waterworks Crossing

A442

HAMPTON LOADE

ALVELEY HALT (Site of)

HIGHLEY

Borle Viaduct

A

A

A

Borle Viaduct

Kinlet Sidings

A442

UPPER ARLEY

Severn Lodge

ARLEY

Victoria Bridge

Trimpley Reservoirs

Eyemore Cutting

Folly Point

B4194

Former Line to Tenbury

NORTHWOOD HALT

B4190

Dowles Jn (Site of)

South Viaduct

A456

KIDDERMINSTER

British Rail

Bewdley North Viaduct

BEWDLEY

Safari Park

FOLEY PARK HALT (closed)

R. Severn

By-Pass Bridge

RIFLE RANGE HALT (Site of)

Bewdley Tunnel

Falling Sands Viaduct

Line Closed)

N

Scale   0   1

S.V.R

Bridgnorth depot

Above left:
The Severn Valley Railway's main locomotive maintenance and repair depot is alongside Bridgnorth station. BR Standard Class 7 Pacific No 70000 *Britannia* poses in the shed yard in August 1978. *D. C. Williams*

Below left:
Great Western locomotives grouped around the water column at Bridgnorth shed in April 1980. *D. C. Williams*

Above:
No 7819 *Hinton Manor* receives a final polish to its nameplate before starting the day's work in April 1980. *D. C. Williams*

Bridgnorth station

Right:
Bridgnorth was approximately half-way between Shrewsbury and Hartlebury on the original Severn Valley Railway, but is now the northern terminus of the Severn Valley line. GWR 0-6-0 No 3205, newly restored to traffic, takes a 'Tenth Anniversary Special' on 15 June 1980 out of platform 2 at Bridgnorth station bound for Bewdley, celebrating 10 years' operation of the preserved Severn Valley Railway. *D. C. Williams*

City of Truro

Above:
Arguably the best known of all GWR engines, No 3440 *City of Truro,* was given a major overhaul at Bridgnorth during 1985. The locomotive had a very brief spell of regular running on the Severn Valley Railway in the spring of 1986 before it was recalled to the National Railway Museum at York. Bringing back memories of its regular usage on the Didcot-Southampton line during the late 1950s, *City of Truro* leaves Bridgnorth on 1 April 1986 with the 15.35 train for Kidderminster. *Phil Waterfield*

Oldbury viaduct

Right:
The viaduct at Oldbury is constructed in brick with five arches, and is of double track width. The severe gales which struck during the 1989-90 winter were responsible for substantial tree damage, one consequence being the creation of a new viewpoint of the viaduct. BR Standard '4' 4-6-0 No 75069 crosses the viaduct on 29 April 1990 with the 15.10 from Bridgnorth to Kidderminster. On the skyline above the locomotive can be seen the domed tower of St Mary's Church in Bridgnorth. *Andrew Bell*

No 8233 at Knowlesands

Left:
Winter photographs at the northern end of the line have generally been restricted to empty stock workings in connection with 'Santa' trains operating on the southern section between Kidderminster and Arley. With cloud advancing slowly from the north, the sun has just risen to provide spectacular lighting on Stanier '8F' No 8233 as it leaves Bridgnorth on 26 November 1989. *Bob Green*

No 34027 at Eardington summit

Right:
After a day of steady rain, rebuilt Bulleid 'West Country' Pacific No 34027 *Taw Valley* brings the 17.00 from Kidderminster to the summit of the 1 in 100 Eardington bank just as a clearance in the western sky bathes the scene in sparkling sunshine on 14 April 1990. Within a few moments the clouds were back again, drawing the curtain on a miserable evening. *Bob Green*

No 3442 on freight

Above:
'K4' 2-6-0 No 3442 *The Great Marquess* looks quite at home with a 24-wagon train on 'heavy freight' weekend 3 June 1990 as it eases down Eardington bank. 3442 was built by the LNER to a Gresley design for operation on the West Highland line from Glasgow to Fort William and Mallaig. Full restoration of the locomotive, which is in terms of tractive effort the most powerful based on the railway, took place at Bridgnorth between 1981 and 1989. Gala weekends on the Severn Valley Railway provide the opportunity to show off the extensive wagon fleet, mainly of Great Western origin, which is maintained by an enthusiastic group of volunteers at Bewdley. *Andrew Bell*

No 5690 Eardington bank

Right:
Beyond the disused Eardington halt, the line passes through a rock cutting for northbound trains before emerging on to a long embankment with a wide, open view from the Highley-Bridgnorth road running alongside. At this point the gradient is 1 in 100 and locomotives can be relied on to work hard on the climb. On 15 April 1989 'Jubilee' No 5690 *Leander* was rostered to work with a rake of seven LMS coaches, thus recreating a scene from the late 1930s, with the 15.55 Kidderminster-Bridgnorth train. The spring of 1989 was very much *Leander's* swan song as shortly afterwards the locomotive succumbed to problems and was withdrawn from service. *Andrew Bell*

Sunset at Hay bridge

Above:
The distinctive outline of a Great Western Small Prairie tank is shown to good effect as No 4566 crosses the embankment just south of Hay bridge, which takes the railway over the Highley-Bridgnorth road. The train is northbound on the late afternoon of 25 October 1987. *Phil Waterfield*

Flying Scotsman

Right:
Over four weekends in the autumn of 1990 Gresley 'A3' Pacific No 4472 *Flying Scotsman* appeared on the Severn Valley Railway. With record receipts taken for the Autumn Gala on 22/23 September the locomotive once again proved its undoubted popularity. Dark clouds loom overhead as *Flying Scotsman* accelerates smartly away from the Sterns slack towards Hay bridge on 7 October 1990 with a train for Bridgnorth. *David Hunt*

Hampton Loade station

Left:
Stanier '8F' 2-8-0 No 8233 takes the through platform at Hampton Loade on 21 June 1977 with a non-stop working from Bridgnorth to Highley. The term 'Loade' indicates a river crossing by means of a ford and, although the ford here has long since gone, the river can still be crossed by ferry. *Andrew Bell*

Prairie tank departure

Above:
GWR Large Prairie tank No 5164 calls at Hampton Loade with a Bridgnorth-Bewdley train on 13 April 1980. The locomotive carries the unlined GWR livery which was applied for its return to service after overhaul in December 1979. *Andrew Bell*

Signalling

The attraction of the Severn Valley Railway is not just in its locomotives and rolling stock. There are many other interesting features to be found along the route not least of which are the signalboxes and signalling equipment. *Above:* The signalbox at Highley is situated opposite the station's single platform and controls a passing loop and sidings. *Left:* Signalmen, like most of the staff on the railway, are volunteers and although they may be rostered for work infrequently nevertheless have to have considerable knowledge and training in order to ensure safe operation of the railway. One of the signalling staff is seen pulling the levers in the box at Bridgnorth station in September 1981. *Both D. C. Williams*

Highley

The station area at Highley provides a good vantage point from which to observe Severn Valley Railway operations, particularly on gala weekends when sidings and loops are extensively used. The station, like Arley, has been successful in winning the Ian Allan Ltd 'Best Restored Station/Railway Heritage Awards' competition. *Right:* The attention to detail in re-creating the country station atmosphere is well illustrated as LMS Stanier '8F' 2-8-0 No 8233 enters the platform with a schools special on 21 June 1977. *Andrew Bell*

Borle viaduct

Above:
Situated south of Highley station is Borle viaduct, a four-arch sandstone
structure which carries the railway over the Borle brook. GWR 'Manor' 4-6-0
No 7812 *Erlestoke Manor* takes the 17.55 train from Bewdley to Bridgnorth
over the viaduct on a very hot Easter Tuesday, 24 April 1984. *Andrew Bell*

Alongside the river

Right:
Although the railway follows the course of the River Severn from Bridgnorth to
Bewdley, the river is actually visible at relatively few locations. Between
Highley and Arley the railway passes Kinlet where sidings once served Kinlet
Colliery, which was closed in 1935. GWR 'Modified Hall' 4-6-0 No 6960
Raveningham Hall has just passed the site of the sidings as it steams alongside
the River Severn on 3 January 1988. *Malcolm Ranieri*

Victoria bridge

Right:
The largest and best known structure on the line is Victoria bridge. It crosses the River Severn by a single span of 200ft made up of four cast-iron ribs. The bridge was completed in 1861, as inscribed on the centre of the arch. The bridge construction is well illustrated in this view taken on 24 April 1988 as Ivatt Class 2 2-6-0 No 46443 crosses with a train for Bridgnorth. *Bob Green*

Over the river

Left:
LMS 'Jinty' 0-6-0T No 47383 crosses the River Severn at Victoria bridge with a local train during the September gala in 1984. There is easy access here to both banks of the River Severn – ideal for walks, or for watching steam trains! *Bob Green*

Trimpley reservoirs

Left:
After the climb from Victoria bridge, southbound trains pass Trimpley. Water is abstracted from the River Severn and stored in the reservoirs here to supplement supplies brought to the Midlands from Wales by an aqueduct which crosses the River Severn nearby. LMS Class 5 4-6-0 No 5000 passes the site with a Bridgnorth-Kidderminster train in the spring of 1987. *David C. Rodgers*

Clun Castle

Right:
The Tyseley-based GWR 'Castle' 4-6-0 No 7029 *Clun Castle* visited the Severn Valley Railway for a short period in the summer of 1982. Here it is seen passing Trimpley with the 'Severn Valley Limited' restaurant car train on 20 June. A four-course luncheon is served on this train, which is a regular feature of Sunday services. *Andrew Bell*

No 43106 enters Bewdley

Left:
A gentle exhaust issues from the chimney of Ivatt '4MT' 2-6-0 No 43106 as it slows for the busy platforms of Bewdley station on 9 December 1984 with a trainload of excited children returning from Santa's grotto at Arley station. Note the fireman holding out the single-line token for the Bewdley North signalman. Although giving the appearance of a double track at this point, the railway at the north end of Bewdley was operated as two single lines in BR days. The track on the left was the Wyre Forest branch from Bewdley to Tenbury Wells and Woofferton, with the Severn Valley line from Shrewsbury coming in on the right. *Andrew Bell*

No 5764 runs round at Bewdley

Right:
GWR 0-6-0PT No 5764 is framed by the footbridge metalwork at Bewdley station in 1976 as it runs round its train prior to a late afternoon return to Bridgnorth. *David C. Rodgers*

Diesels on the Valley

Several diesel locomotives are based on the Severn Valley Railway. Although none are regularly rostered for service trains they do get a chance to show their paces on special 'Diesel Weekends'. One very popular feature of such weekends is the wide variety of visiting engines which appear. *Above:* On 7 May 1988 General Motors Class 59 No 59001 *Yeoman Endeavour* makes an extremely rare appearance on a passenger train as it runs into Bewdley. The locomotive is privately owned by Foster Yeoman Ltd, and is normally operated on stone trains in the South and West of England. *Bryan Hicks*

One of the SVR's own fleet of diesels, Sulzer-engined Bo-Bo No D7633, ambles through Bewdley station with a Kidderminster-Highley goods train during a celebration gala on 23 June 1990. The locomotive was built in 1965 by Beyer Peacock at Gorton and came to the Severn Valley in 1988. *Andrew Bell*

Local train at Bewdley

Left:
Bewdley station was, in former times, an important interchange with junctions to the north and south of the station. Nowadays it is the administrative headquarters of the Severn Valley Railway, as well as the most important intermediate station between Kidderminster and Bridgnorth. LMS Jinty 0-6-0T No 47383 pauses in Platform 3 with a two-coach local from Kidderminster to Arley on 23 June 1990. *Andrew Bell*

Special working

Above:
BR Standard '4' 4-6-0 No 75069 passes the fine display of signals by Bewdley South signalbox on 2 June 1990. The train carries a perishables headlamp code and incorporates fruit vans as it runs from Highley to Kidderminster during a 'heavy freight' gala weekend. *Andrew Bell*

Great Western freight

Above:
The GWR '28XX' class was the first design of 2-8-0 wheel arrangement to be built in Britain. Their purpose was the haulage of heavy mineral trains, and the Churchward design was so successful that they operated for over half a century in that capacity. Locomotive No 2857 looks quite at home making light work of a demonstration freight train climbing to Bewdley tunnel on 22 May 1988. *Paul Stratford*

Bewdley tunnel

Right:
The 480yd-long Bewdley tunnel takes the railway beneath a sandstone outcrop on the edge of Kidderminster. The tunnel curves towards its western portal and lies on a 1 in 100 gradient downhill towards Bewdley. Unusually GWR 'Hall' 4-6-0 No 4930 *Hagley Hall* still has steam on leaving the tunnel with the 14.20 from Kidderminster on 27 October 1984, picking up speed after a permanent way slack on the eastern approach to the tunnel. *Andrew Bell*

Kidderminster Loop

Left:
Stanier Class 5 4-6-0 No 5000, looking immaculate with a train of maroon BR
Mk 1 coaches, storms the 1 in 100 gradient from Bewdley to Foley Park with
empty stock from Kidderminster on the morning of 30 October 1988. The
heathland sprinkled with silver birch trees on this stretch of the Severn Valley
Railway has very much of a Scottish atmosphere about it. No 5000 which
belongs to the National Collection operated on the railway between 1979 and
1988. *Andrew Bell*

Express motive power

Above:
Carrying the 'Elizabethan' headboard, Gresley 'A4' Pacific No 60009 bursts out
of Bewdley tunnel during a run-past for the cameras of Central Television on
Friday 16 February 1990. Following a major overhaul at Bridgnorth locomotive
works the 'A4' had extensive running-in trials on the railway before returning to
Scotland to take part in the Forth Bridge centenary celebrations. *Bryan Hicks*

Foley Park

Left:
On 15 December 1984 GWR 'Manor' 4-6-0 No 7812 *Erlestoke Manor* passes the sidings which served the local Kidderminster sugar beet factory between 1925 and 1980. A passenger halt also existed at Foley Park in BR days, but has never been used by Severn Valley Railway trains. There is currently very little evidence of either the sidings or the halt at this site. *Andrew Bell*

Falling Sands

Right:
For trains leaving Kidderminster the first major feature on the line is Falling Sands viaduct, 132yd long and spanning both the River Stour and the Staffordshire & Worcestershire Canal. The canal fishermen appear quite impassive as GWR 'Hall' 4-6-0 No 4930 *Hagley Hall* crosses high above them with a Kidderminster-Arley 'Santa' train on 8 December 1984. *Phil Waterfield*